# CHRISTMAS

An Easy-Read Holiday Book

# CHRISTMAS

## by Cass R. Sandak

### Illustrations by Cynthia Pickard

FRANKLIN WATTS
New York/London/Toronto/Sydney
1980

To my nephew
**Jeffery William Sandak**
for his first Christmas

**R.L. 2.9 Spache Revised Formula**

Library of Congress Cataloging in Publication Data

Sandak, Cass R.
  Christmas.

  (Easy-read holiday book)
  Includes index.
  SUMMARY: Traces the pre-Christian origins of the
Christmas celebration and discusses the customs asso-
ciated with this holiday since the birth of Christ.
  1. Christmas—Juvenile literature. [1. Christmas]
I. Pickard, Cynthia, 1947-        II. Title.   III. Series.
GT4985.S18            394.2′68282            80-11114
ISBN 0-531-04147-6

Christmas is almost always the happiest day of the year. Children like to think of it as their own holiday. But for everyone it is a very special time.

At Christmas, we follow old customs. We feel the magic of the season. And we try to care more deeply for others.

Christmas is filled with wonderful things to see, hear, smell, and taste. And there is the special warmth that Christmas brings—a mixture of joy, love, and peace.

Christmas gets its name from a special service or mass held in churches on Christmas Day. **Christ's Mass,** or Christmas, celebrates the birth of Jesus Christ.

At Christmas, we remember the beautiful story of Jesus' birth, or **nativity** (nuh-TIV-ah-tee).

Long ago in the Holy Land, the angel **Gabriel** (GAY-bree-ul) appeared to Mary. He told her that she would be the mother of Jesus. Then Mary and her husband Joseph went to **Bethlehem** (BETH-lee-hem). The city was so crowded that they had to stay in a stable. There Mary gave birth to Jesus and laid him in a **manger** (MAIN-jur). A manger is a feedbox where farm animals eat their hay.

Angels came down from heaven to tell the shepherds in the fields about Jesus' birth. They brought a message of peace on earth. A bright star appeared in the sky above Jesus' birthplace. Three Wise Men — or kings — who studied the heavens, followed the star's light to the stable. They presented the baby Jesus with gifts of gold, **frankincense** (FRANK-in-sense), a sweet-smelling incense, and **myrrh** (MUR), a bitter scent.

We remember the visit of the three Wise Men on **Epiphany** (ee-PIF-uh-nee), January 6. Epiphany comes from a Greek word that means "to show." At Bethlehem, Jesus first showed himself to the world. Epiphany is also called Twelfth Night. It marks the end of the Twelve Days of Christmas.

At Christmas, many families set up figures in a **crèche** (KRESH), or manger scene, in their homes. Saint Francis of **Assisi** (ah-SEE-see) started this custom. It reminds people of Jesus' birth in the stable. Saint Francis used live animals and real people in his crèche.

Animals were the first to see Jesus in the stable at Bethlehem. This was thought to be a sign of blessing from God. In some countries, farm animals are given special food at Christmastime. Some people scatter seeds for birds to nibble.

Jesus was born about two thousand years ago, though we do not know the exact number of years. For more than three hundred years after his birth, no one kept a careful count of the years. Few people in those days knew or cared about Christmas.

Now, we number our years from Christ's birth. Perhaps you have seen the letters **B.C.** or **A.D.** next to a year. B.C. means "Before Christ" and includes all the years before Jesus was born. A.D. stands for two Latin words, **Anno Domini** (ANN-oh DOM-ee-nee), that mean "In the year of Our Lord." This means all the years after Jesus' birth.

Before Jesus was born, most people were **pagans** (PAY-gunz). This means that they prayed to the sun, the moon, and many different gods of nature.

Late December can be a cold, dark time of the year. December 21 is the shortest day of the year. But by December 25, the days get longer again. The pagans of the Roman Empire called December 25 the "Birthday of the Sun." During their winter holidays, they gave each other dolls, candles, and evergreen branches.

No one knows the exact day when Jesus was born. Some early churches celebrated Jesus' birth on different dates through the year—in March or May or December! By about 325 A.D., many of the people in the Roman Empire had become Christians. A few years later, Pope Julian chose December 25 as the date for Christmas. Some people even thought that this was the actual day Jesus was born.

Late December had been a holiday time for hundreds of years. The pagan Romans had celebrated their **Saturnalia** (sat-ur-NAIL-yah) at this time of the year. And Jewish people have held their eight-day **Hanukkah** (HAHN-uh-kah) celebration since about one hundred and fifty years before the birth of Christ.

As Christianity spread through Europe and to other parts of the world, new customs were added to old ones. Many pagan customs were kept. All parts of the world gave traditions of their own to make Christmas as we know it today.

Over the years, Christmas has been celebrated in many different ways. But everywhere the joy of Christ's birth and the happy customs of the season are important parts of the holiday.

Weeks before December 25, people begin preparing for Christmas. Families bake cakes and cookies. They put up decorations and wrap presents. Stores set up displays to attract shoppers.

Sometimes the four weeks before Christmas are called **Advent.** In many churches, candles set in evergreen wreaths are lighted on each of the four Sundays of Advent.

Children in Germany often have Advent calendars with little shuttered windows in them. Each day they open one more window. They find a surprise inside—a picture of a toy or a holiday scene. Somehow it seems to make the long wait for Christmas pass more quickly.

Christmas is a time when families and friends like to be together and share the joy of the season. Often people travel a long way to be with their loved ones during the holiday. Grandparents who live far away may come to visit their grandchildren.

We try to keep in touch with people we care about even if we cannot be with them. We make long distance telephone calls and send Christmas cards, letters, and gifts. Christmas is a time to remember the people we love.

**18**

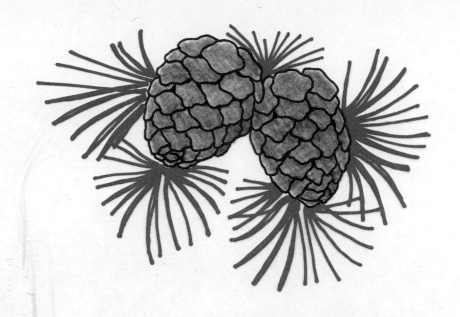

As December 25 gets closer, people set up Christmas trees. The story of the Christmas tree comes to us from Germany.

Hundreds of years ago, the Germans were pagans. Each winter they sacrificed a young person in front of an oak tree. Around the year 750 A.D., a missionary named **Boniface** (BONN-eh-face) came from Rome to teach the people about Christ. He told them to bring pine trees into their homes as a sign of change from the old ways. The oak tree had meant death. But evergreen trees stand for life. Even in winter their needles stay green.

Slowly, Christmas trees became popular. Early trees were trimmed with paper, cloth, nuts, and metal foil. About five hundred years ago, the religious leader Martin Luther put candles on his Christmas tree. He thought they looked like the stars on Christmas night. We still put strings of lights on our Christmas trees.

About 1835, the first Christmas tree in America was decorated. A few years later in England, Queen Victoria decorated a tree at **Windsor** (WIN-zer) Castle. That is where the British royal family spends Christmas. Soon Christmas trees became very popular. Nearly every home in the United States, Great Britain, Germany, and France had one.

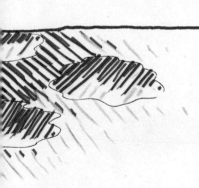

Many people put up wreaths and other decorations. Decorating with evergreen branches and special plants is one of the oldest parts of the Christmas holiday.

In our homes, we may hang a piece of **mistletoe** (MISS-ul-toe) from the ceiling or over a doorway at Christmas. Anyone who stands under it may be kissed. For each kiss, one of the white berries from the mistletoe should be plucked off the branch. When all the berries are gone, the kissing should stop. If you are shy, you should not go under the mistletoe!

Long ago, the **Druid** (DROO-id) priests who lived in France and the British Isles thought mistletoe was a holy plant. It grows high off the ground on trees. In winter, mistletoe looks bright green among the dark branches of the forest. Because it was used for ancient magic, mistletoe almost never appears in church decorations.

Holly was used by the ancient Northern Europeans at their winter festival. But its shiny green leaves and bright red berries made holly a popular Christmas decoration. The spiky leaves of holly reminded some people of Christ's crown of thorns.

The red flowers of the **poinsettia**
(poyn-SETT-uh) plant come from Mexico.
There it is called the "Flower of the Holy Night."
An American named Poinsett introduced the plant
to the United States.

Shopping, cooking, and decorating fill the busy days before Christmas. But the night before Christmas, Christmas Eve, marks the true beginning of the holiday.

On Christmas Eve, many families gather for a special meal. In Poland, the Christmas Eve dinner begins when the first star appears in the sky. People in many European countries eat fish. Some people have spinach because they think that Mary ate it the night that Jesus was born.

Christmas Eve is rich in traditions. Many people light candles or make fires in their fireplaces. In earlier times, the burning of a big **Yule** log was one of the most important Christmas customs. Long ago, Northern Europeans called their winter festival Yule. The Yule log was supposed to burn as long as the festival lasted. This would bring good luck.

In France, a festive supper follows midnight mass on Christmas Eve. Friends and relatives feast until dawn. A cake made in the shape of a Yule log is often served.

Many churches hold candlelight services on Christmas Eve. These often begin at midnight. Bells are rung and joyful hymns are sung.

Music is an important part of Christmas celebrations. Hundreds of Christmas songs come from all over the world. The first Christmas songs were hymns. The Latin words of "O Come All Ye Faithful" are almost as old as Christmas itself.

In the Middle Ages, Christmas **carols** (KAH-rulls) became popular. The word carol means a round dance. Often, carolers danced in the street. Musicians sometimes played the flute or the drum. In Spain, all-night dancing is still a part of Christmas Eve. In many countries, carol singers go from house to house. Or they may gather around a lighted Christmas tree in a park.

Giving presents has always been a part of Christmas. Even before Christianity, the Romans gave each other gifts during Saturnalia. The Wise Men brought rich presents to the newborn Jesus. Today, families and friends exchange gifts at Christmas to show their love and affection.

Sometimes the gifts are opened on Christmas Eve. But on Christmas morning, children usually open the presents that Santa Claus brought during the night. The Dutch who settled New York in the 1600s brought this custom to America. In Holland and Belgium, Santa is called **Saint Nicholas** (NICK-uh-luss). He rides a horse when he visits children on Saint Nicholas Day, December 6. This marks the beginning of the Christmas season in these countries.

The real Saint Nicholas was a bishop who lived more than sixteen hundred years ago. He would help the poor by secretly leaving gifts for them in their houses at night. Now Santa is said to ride through the air in a sleigh pulled by eight reindeer. He climbs down the chimney to leave gifts for American children on the night before Christmas. In Great Britain, children eagerly await Father Christmas, who is really the same as Santa Claus. In France, he is called **Père Noël** (pair no-WELL).

In many homes, children hang up stockings on Christmas Eve. In the morning, they hope to find them filled with fruit, gingerbread, and other small gifts. In many places around the world, shoes are used instead of stockings.

In Great Britain, the day after Christmas is called Boxing Day. People show their thanks by giving money to those who have provided services during the year. This money used to be given in boxes.

January 1 comes within the twelve days of Christmas. New Year's Day is the time for gift giving in some parts of France and Scotland. The familiar New Year's Eve song, "Auld Lang Syne"—which means "Old Times"—came from Scotland. The Scottish people have their biggest celebration then.

In many Southern European and Latin American countries, presents are given on Twelfth Night, January 6. Mexican children receive their gifts on that day or on Christmas.

In Mexico, a **piñata** (peen-YAH-tah) is hung from the ceiling. This is a large pottery jar filled with small gifts. Sometimes it is shaped like an animal. Blindfolded children try to break the piñata with a stick. When it breaks, they collect their gifts.

In some countries, children are told that the Wise Men bring their gifts on Twelfth Night. In Italy, a kind old witch named **Befana** (bay-FAH-nuh) brings them. In still other countries, the gifts are said to be brought by angels or by the Christ Child himself.

After the gaily wrapped packages have been opened, Christmas is a day to have fun. Children enjoy playing with new toys or dolls. Parents try to relax.

On Christmas Day, most families gather for the traditional Christmas dinner. Many people have a turkey or ham. Sometimes roast goose is served at Christmas dinner.

We have some special foods only at Christmas —fruitcake, plum pudding, and mince pie. Plum pudding is really a rich cake filled with nuts and candied fruit. Raisins are used instead of plums. Mince pies are also made from raisins, fruit, and nuts that are minced, or chopped up very small. These things were first made in Great Britain. Decorated cookies and fancy gingerbread houses came from different European countries.

Christmas in England four hundred years ago was the merriest the world has ever seen. In the time of England's first Queen Elizabeth, Christmas was celebrated with weeks of merrymaking in the castles and large houses.

The highlight was the feast on Christmas Day. Servers marched into the great hall with a roasted boar's head. Sometimes cooks roasted a peacock, and then sewed it back into its skin and feathers. This was brought to the table by a noble lady. There were countless pies and other steaming dishes.

The custom of drinking **wassail** (WAH-sull) also came from England. Wassail means "Good Health!" It is a punch made from hot spiced wine. Or it may be a drink like eggnog. When people drink wassail, all their quarrels should stop.

The southern United States was settled by British people who kept many of the customs of the old English Christmas. On the great southern plantations, Christmas lasted for many days. A Yule log burned all through the celebration, and both rich and poor people were welcome. Huge Christmas cakes filled with fruits and nuts were baked. George Washington's wife Martha needed forty eggs to make her Christmas cake!

But Christmas was not always a holiday. The Puritans in Great Britain and those who settled in New England were very strict. They did not celebrate Christmas. Little by little, however, more fun-loving groups spread the holiday. By the 1800s, Christmas was celebrated all over the United States.

The American Indians did not celebrate
Christmas until European missionaries taught them
about Christ. Then the Indians adopted some of
the customs of the settlers around them. But they
also brought many of their own traditions to the
holiday. Beautiful Christmas songs tell of the
Great Spirit who came down from the sky to be
born in a forest hut. This is how the Indians saw
the birth of Jesus.

For hundreds of years, kindness and charity have been shown at Christmas. At the old English holiday feasts, all were welcome. In many places, it is still good luck to see a stranger on Christmas. In Poland, an extra place is set at the table for an unexpected guest.

Christmas is a time of peace. People who are angry with each other sometimes make up. If countries are at war, they try to stop fighting. For at least a few days there is peace on earth.

Charity is more freely given at Christmas. People leave baskets of food for the needy. Groups visit prisons, hospitals, and homes for the aged to sing carols and pass out gifts. Others give clothing and toys to families who do not have enough money to buy them.

Sharing with others shows the true spirit of the season. Around the world people make special efforts to see that everyone has A MERRY CHRISTMAS!

# INDEX